This I Know For Sure...

A story of how God answered a
couple's prayer through an adopted child

May you be assured
that you were created
with significance +
purpose...
Blessings,
Karen + Rob

Written by
Karen Capson

Illustrated by Ashley Lanni

Copyright © 2013 Karen Capson
All rights reserved.

ISBN: 1480180149
ISBN 13: 9781480180147

Library of Congress Control Number: 2012920404
CreateSpace Independent Publishing Platform, North Charleston, SC

This book adopted by:

_____

~ Dedicated to ~

My Lord and Savior, Jesus Christ ~
I give You all the credit and glory for the many blessings and opportunities
You have so graciously bestowed upon me in this lifetime.
Philippians 4:13 ~ "I can do all this through Him who gives me strength."

My husband, Greg ~
There is no other I'd have chosen to share my life's journey with, than you.
Thank you for being my rock and devoted better half.
You are an amazing partner and role model to our daughter.
I love you dearly…

My precious gift, Madison ~
May your faith stand strong in knowing that you were wonderfully
and masterfully made by God, and are loved beyond
measure by your mom and dad.

~ A Special Note from the Author ~

Parents, may this children's story evoke warm memories for you, while promoting impactful and heartfelt dialogue between you and your child. The reading level of this book is purposely elevated above that which your child might be able to read on his or her own, to encourage the need for your participation. Find a quiet, cozy spot to read the story aloud to your child. Take time to "paws" and reflect when you come to the kitty paw prints, scattered throughout the storyline. Encourage your child to read these "conversation starters" to *you*, providing him or her an opportunity to ask questions about the adoption. Reassure your child of any concerns and emotions he or she may have, and be open to elaborate on connected topics that may arise. Conclude your time together with a family-centered activity or game. You will find additional tips and activities for celebrating adoption and family in the back of this book. You may also wish to extend your sentiments to your child in written form, by completing the journal prompts located on the "Fill Up My Love Cup" pages. Your child will be able to read, over and over again, just how deep your love runs for him or her as you express your fondest memories of the adoption, how the child has blessed your life, and your most sincere desires for his or her future. May your exchanges together be fulfilling, and lead to the assurance that your child's existence is nothing shy of a miracle from God.

Blessings,

Karen

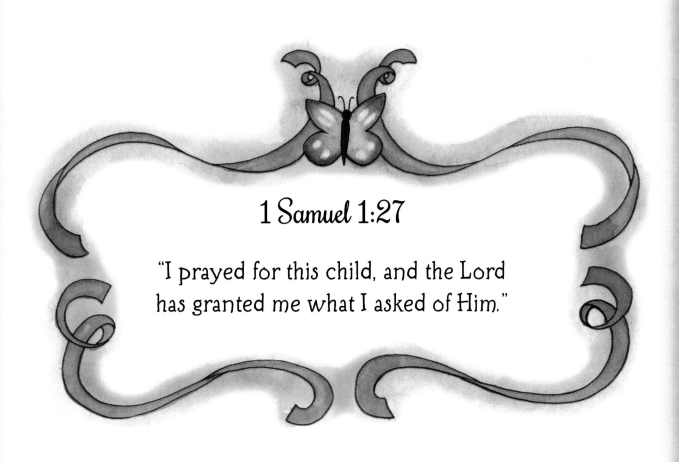

1 Samuel 1:27

"I prayed for this child, and the Lord has granted me what I asked of Him."

It was no ordinary Saturday morning, and Madison stood in her closet, carefully inspecting each dress on the rack. She contemplated which would be the *perfect* one to wear for her special celebration dinner, that evening.

"Have you made your final decision yet, Sweetheart?" Mom asked, knowing that whatever Madison selected would be perfectly suited for the occasion, and would very likely contain a splash of baby pink, *by far* Madi's favorite color. "What about the one with all the different-colored butterflies on it?" Mom asked, pointing to the beautiful, frilly garment on the purple hanger. It had just enough layers of crinoline underneath it to make twirling around oh so perfect. Mom reached beyond Madi to pull the patterned dress from the closet, knelt down in front of her, and draped the dress against her torso. "Grandma Peggy would simply *love* this one," Mom shared, delightedly.

"How do you know she'd like it?" Madi asked.

Mom responded, "You see those beautifully colored butterfly magnets over there, attached to your bulletin board? Well, those once belonged to your grandma Peggy before she went on to Heaven. I know she would be so pleased that you now have them. She took great joy in collecting anything with butterflies on it and adored, just like you, the same soft shades of yellow, pink, and blue. In fact, every time she visited your father and me on her trips from Canada, she would wear pretty pastel tops that remind me very much of the colored butterflies I see in this dress. If she were alive today, *surely* she'd tell you how much she liked this dress too, and how beautiful you look in it."

"Well then," Madi said confidently, "that's, *for sure*, the one! It's the perfect dress to wear for my Adoption Day party tonight!" Madi couldn't explain it, but somehow she felt it in her heart that what Mom had said was true... Grandma Peggy would have, indeed, approved of her dress selection, and thought she looked just like a little princess.

"Daddy's mom may not be here to celebrate this special day with us," Mommy continued, "but *this I know for sure...* she's been smiling down on you from Heaven ever since you were born, and is in every way a part of each of our family celebrations!"

When is my Adoption Day?
What are some of our family's traditions?

Psalm 37:4

"Delight yourself in the Lord,
and He will give you the desires of your heart."

Madi wandered into her parents' bedroom to find her cat, Angel, resting on the orange blanket that lay folded at the foot of their bed. As she would do every morning, Madi greeted her furry friend with an upbeat, "Hi, Angel!" to which the dark-striped tabby cat would respond with an outburst of short, repetitive meow sounds. Angel seemed to make those Morse-code "meows" only when greeting her favorite little buddy, Madison. It was as if they had their own unique language, one that only *they* could understand.

Their daily ritual continued with

Madison asking Angel if she

was thirsty and wanted some water,

leading her into her parents' bathroom

and turning on,

ever so slowly,

the bathtub faucet

from which Angel would drink.

After standing up

on her hind legs for a brief moment,

Angel cautiously jumped up

onto the side of the tub

and began lapping up her tummy's fill

from the steady stream of water.

As Mom entered the bathroom to begin her own morning routine, she was forced to quickly step aside as a startled Angel ran swiftly from the bathroom and straight down the hallway with lightning speed and prowess. Madi often imagined that she was an exotic cat trainer, able to tame even the "wild ways" of her pet, Angel.

"Mom..." Madi asked, turning off the faucet, "Was Angel adopted just like me?"

"Well," Mom responded, "while Mommy and Daddy were waiting for God to bring you into our lives, we decided we wanted to share our love with a pet by adopting a kitty and giving her a safe home, so we could care for her and nurture her. We decided to name her Angel, because she was like our little 'Angel,' helping us to not think *too* much about the hole we felt in our hearts; a hole that we knew could only be filled by a child to call our very own."

"Did I fill that hole, Mommy?" Madi asked.

"Oh Madi, you were the absolute *perfect* puzzle piece to make our hearts whole again and complete our family picture. Do you realize that God created every bit of you… from your head to your toes, your unique personality, your special gifts and talents, and even your love of animals? He distinctly designed you to fit perfectly into our family. He handcrafted every trait of you specifically and especially to be our very own, one-of-a-kind child. Funny thing is…not only did you *fill* the vacant spot we had in our hearts, but you caused our "love cup" to spill over, like that of a running faucet. You are abundantly *more* than we could have ever asked for or dreamed of in a biological child."

Madi asked, "Is that why you say, I may not have come from your tummy, but I grew from your heart?"

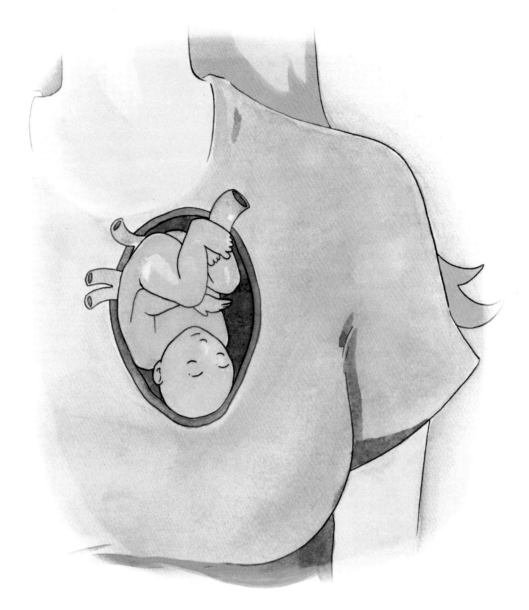

Mom replied, *"This I know for sure...* God couldn't have chosen a more perfect child for our family than you, Buttercup!"

How did I grow in your heart?
Do I know anyone else who is adopted?

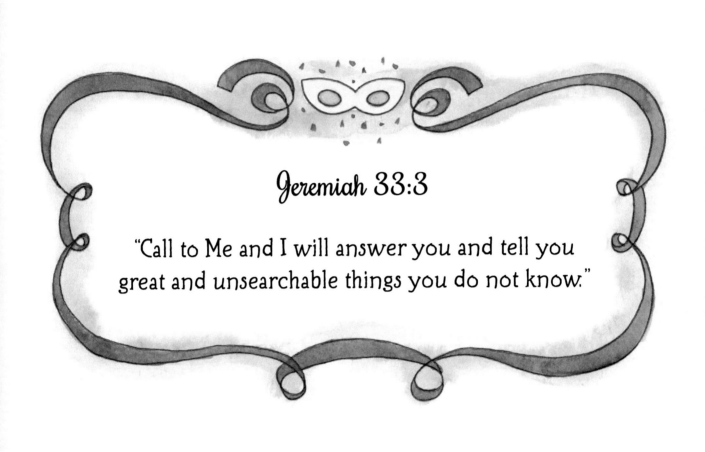

Jeremiah 33:3

"Call to Me and I will answer you and tell you great and unsearchable things you do not know."

$\mathcal{D}$ ownstairs, Dad was preparing breakfast and the house filled with the smell of warm cinnamon-swirl rolls...the kind that Madi simply couldn't resist! She loved helping to spread the gooey, white icing across the tops of each roll once they emerged from the oven. She got such joy from watching the icing run down the sides of the hot treat and land on the tips of her delicate fingers. She couldn't help but lick off the drippings, starting at her thumb and working her way down the row, finishing at her little pinky.

Dad had already begun to set the table, and once Madi had finished making concentric swirls on the tops of each round puck (that's what Daddy called them), she sat down at the table, eagerly waiting for Mom to emerge from upstairs and partake in the morning's delicacy.

After placing a glass of juice and a napkin at each seat, Dad proceeded to walk around the table, setting a plate on each placemat. Madi's eyes shined brightly as she realized that *her* plate was different than the plain old white ones her mom and dad were going to eat from. Dad read the words painted on the large, colorful plate aloud to Madison, as he kissed her gently on her forehead, "You are special today and always," it read. "Mommy painted this plate, years before you were born, in hopes that *one day* she would have a child to share it with on special days, such as today. From what I understand, Nana, too, has a special plate she used to serve meals on from time to time for Mommy and Aunt Lisa." Madi carefully inspected the details of the plate, running her fingers around the raised white dots along the outside rim. She then carefully turned over the heavy plate to reveal, in perfect handwriting, "November 2001."

"But, Mommy made this four years before I was even *born*, Daddy... How could she *possibly* have known when she painted it, that one day I would be eating off it?" Madi seemed a bit perplexed.

Dad responded, "She had strong faith, my love...she had faith in knowing that God would grant her deepest, innermost wishes of not only becoming a mother some day, but being able to pass along the childhood traditions of *her* youth to her son or daughter."

"Is *that* why my middle name is 'Faith'?" Madison inquired.

"Why yes, Madi Faith, it is," Dad smiled. "God tested our patience for eight years after we were married, but He used that time to grow us as a couple, test our faith in Him, and He ultimately helped Mommy and Daddy to become better parents because of it."

Just then, Mom walked into the kitchen, beaming in delight as she inhaled the sweet aroma that filled the air. As the three sat down, they reached across the table to one another, clasped hands in a united circle, bowed their heads, and Mom began to pray, "Heavenly Father, we give You thanks today and *every* day for the miracle of our daughter, Madison. We thank You for answered prayers and the joy that comes from knowing that if we ask it of You, in Your perfect timing, *all* things are possible. Bless this food to the nourishment of our minds, bodies, and souls...In Your Son's Holy Name, Amen."

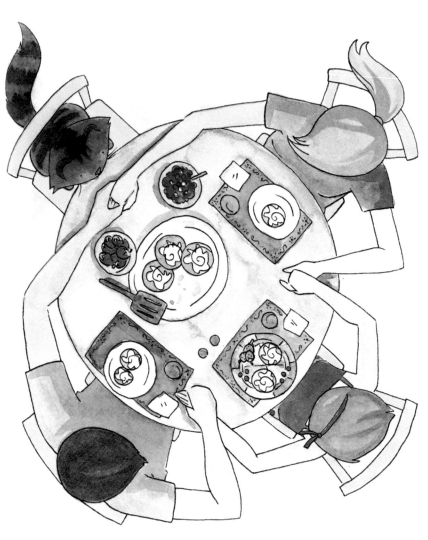

"Mmmm, mmmmm, Madison! These cinnamon rolls sure look delicious!" Dad exclaimed. *"This I know for sure...* just as God rewarded our patience with the blessing of you, so too will our taste buds be rewarded for their patience! Dig in, family!"

What makes me special?
How did I get my name?

Jeremiah 32:27

"I am the Lord, the God of all mankind.
Is anything too hard for Me?"

After breakfast, Madi headed upstairs while Mom and Dad continued to clean up the remaining dishes. She walked over to the bookcase that housed the many photo albums that Mom had kept so neatly chronicled, and pulled out the first in its row: a thick, pink scrapbook with a monogrammed "C" on the cover. She sat down on the plush carpet, folded her legs into a pretzel and opened it up to the first page.

She read the words, "Madison Faith Capson (Book #1)." She turned the page and paused for a moment. She carefully studied the two photographs displayed, both of a tiny baby who appeared to be crying after apparently having her umbilical cord cut. She also took close notice of the bright purple gloves on the hands of the nurse caring for the baby. She then read the handwriting to the left of the photos, "Friday, November 18th at 11:21 a.m." Beneath that it read, "6 pounds, 13.3 ounces, 20 ¾ inches."

"That's me!" Madi thought. As she continued flipping through the many plastic-coated pages, she would occasionally pause for brief moments to admire the photos that caught her interest. She *especially* loved the set of photos showing her mom and dad wearing baseball hats.

Dad's was dark blue with pink cursive writing that read, "Daddy of Madison Faith," and Mommy's was in pink, *of course*, with white writing that read, "Mommy of Madison Faith." Madi recalled her mother telling her the story of how she and Daddy knew that they were going to adopt a baby girl, but wanted to keep the name a surprise from everyone until she was born. Her parents strutted down the hall to the waiting room, where the family awaited her arrival, and announced that their baby girl was healthy and simply perfect! They flashed their hats for everyone to see the name they had chosen for their little miracle. "How proud and happy they both looked on that special day," Madi thought, "...my BIRTH-day!"

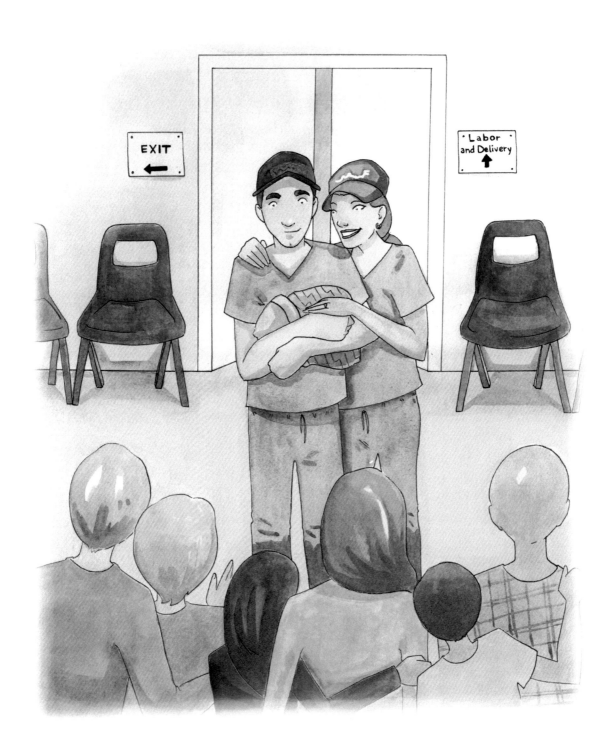

Slowly turning page by page, Madi encountered photos of her aunt Lisa holding a bundled baby, with obvious tears of joy in her eyes; her nana, her granddaddy, and even photos of her two cousins, Zach and Lauren (looking much younger, though). The pair were standing in front of their garage door, arms raised toward a large hanging, hand-crafted banner, which read, "WELCOME MADI!! WE LOVE YOU!!" That was Thanksgiving morning and Madi's first day after coming home from the hospital. Madi thought again to herself, "Wow...Mommy and Daddy weren't the *only* ones waiting for me to be a part of this family!"

Without a doubt, Madi could see the excitement, joy, and pride everyone displayed from their gestures in each photo. It was as if she was personally experiencing her "firsts" all over again.

"Ten Days Old - First Hockey Game with Daddy," "First Bath," "First Christmas Present," "First Visit to Canada" to meet her auntie Theresea and uncle Darrell,

"First New Year's Eve" (at another hockey game), "First Valentine's Day," and there it was...Madi stopped again, this time to read in her mom's handwriting, "Madi Gras Adoption Day – February 23rd."

Mom soon joined Madison upstairs and found her lying on the floor amongst a scattered array of pictures. It was obvious that Madi was engrossed in the photographic account of her first year of life. "I bet you don't have any recollection of when those photos were taken, do you? To me, those memories are as fresh in my mind today as they were back then," Mom shared.

"There are so many people in these pictures, Mommy...some I know, and some I don't know, but they all seem so happy to be holding me and hugging me."

"You've got that right!" Mom exclaimed. "I've got something special I want to show you—I'll be right back." Mom disappeared momentarily into the bedroom and, after moving some boxes around on shelves, she emerged again, holding a small, bound notebook in her right hand. She sat down on the floor next to Madi, who quickly sat up in anticipation, to see what treasure her mom had uncovered. "Inside this book," Mom began, "are many letters, written by close friends and family of both Mommy and Daddy.

In each letter, you can read just how much everyone was praying for you to come into our lives, how wanted you were (even before we had met you), and how blessed we felt that God had specifically chosen Stacie to carry you in her tummy for us, when I could not.

She loved you so much, and knew deep down in her heart that God created you with a purpose and a plan; and that your life's course was to be fulfilled through your growing up in our family and in our home. On the day you were born, we gave Stacie a copy of this same book of letters, so she could be continually reminded of our appreciation to her for the abundant gift she gave to us that special day in November."

"And 'Madi Gras' is the day we celebrate when I officially got my last name from you and Daddy?" Madi added.

"Well, that too, but it is also the day to remember the promise that we made to you six years ago—the promise to love you without fail, to protect you and guide you, and to always be your supportive parents for as long as we live. We not only made this solemn vow to you, but we made it to God, as well. *This I know for sure...* As your parents, it is His plan for us to fulfill *our* purpose by helping you live out *yours* and carrying out His desires for you from birth."

How did you know you wanted to adopt?
Did you meet my birth parents?

Ecclesiastes 3:1

"There is a time for everything,
and a season for every activity under Heaven."

Later that afternoon, Madi could hear the faint sound of her father's voice from outside her bedroom window, calling for her to come down and join him in the front yard. On an occasional Saturday morning, Madi would help her father while he fiddled around with the direction of the sprinkler heads, watered and trimmed the potted trees on each side of the driveway, or simply picked stray weeds from the manicured nursery beds. He didn't get a chance to work outdoors as much as he would like, so when the weather permitted and he had no other responsibilities that morning, he'd jump at the chance to get out to his private sanctuary. It gave him an opportunity to slow down, take in some fresh air, and marvel at the fruits of his labor. He enjoyed seeing, first-hand, how the plants under his care had grown and prospered since his last visit with them.

"Hey, Sweetie!" Dad called to Madi, as she stepped out from the cover of the front porch and onto the lawn. "Want to help Daddy with a little project?"

"Sure," she replied…. "What are we gonna do?" Before he even had a chance to answer her, Madi had already maneuvered her way through the garage maze and grabbed her watering can and pink metal bucket from the shelf. In it, she carried her miniature rake and shovel, and a pair of "ladylike" garden gloves, though she was rarely seen *wearing* them. If there was one thing that Madison had no hesitation about, it was the opportunity to play in the dirt. Her mother often cringed at the thought of all the gunk Madi would get trapped beneath her fingernails. But after she witnessed first-hand her daughter's sheer delight in making mud pies, she eventually conceded that a long bath soak was an easy remedy for cleaning up the mess.

Madi followed her dad through the white picket gate at the side of their house and into their backyard. She continued walking in her father's wake, until he paused to glance down at the large patches of dried grass, which Madi thought, resembled the spotted coat of a cheetah. "See these areas of strawlike thatch in the grass?" Daddy asked her. "I need your help raking out the dead areas, so we can spread a thin layer of topsoil over them. The enriched dirt will help prepare these bare patches for when spring comes. The hearty grass surrounding them will extend their roots toward the soil, encouraging newer and healthier grass to grow in place of what now appears barren."

Madi and her father worked closely alongside one another like two peas in a pod, sharing stories and taking turns cracking funny jokes. It was amazing to Mom how similar they both were in that respect—quick-witted, with a clever sense of humor. "Like father, like daughter," Mom often thought.

In about an hour's time, they had cleared away the old remnants of thatch, revealing a fresh new foundation beneath. They took a momentary breather to step back, admire their feat, and soak in the sense of accomplishment they both felt from working so diligently. "So, how long until we see the new green grass grow, Daddy?" Madi asked.

"Well, it's hard to say, Honey," Dad responded. "I don't know the exact time frame, but I *do* know that it will eventually sprout in God's perfect timing. You see, He leaves it to us to prepare the ground, fertilize it, water it, and continue caring for it… until, ultimately, He determines the right time to unveil His marvelous results!

They began to sweep off the dirt from their hands and clothing, when Madi yelled, "Look, Daddy, look!" She squealed with delight…, "A cricket!" She pointed to the small brown insect perched atop the nearby fence post. "Papa George must know that today's my special day, too!" she said with a laugh. She moved in for a closer look, remembering fondly how he would lovingly refer to her as his little "cricket." Papa George really had a way of making her feel special, especially when he would flash his toothy smile and send a quick wink in her direction. After his passing a few years ago, she believed that every cricket sighting was her papa's way of sending her a "God wink," straight from Heaven.

Daddy, too, felt the excitement and significance of seeing that cricket in their backyard. "You know, Madi…it is Mommy's and my every prayer that we may continue to help you develop the interests and talents that God has uniquely given you. We know that in His perfect timing, He will abundantly bless your hard work and use your life experiences as a means to nourish the individuals in your life's path. We hope that you'll continue to speak freely and openly about your own adoption story; so that, in time, like the grass, God may use you as an example to inspire and encourage growth in others. *This I know for sure...* If you remain firmly planted in your faith and immersed in His word and truth, He will use your gifts and talents to help others foster their own. Someday, I pray you will lead your *own* children, biological or adopted, to know the Lord as you do, and encourage *them* to dream, far beyond that which they ever envisioned was possible!"

The two exchanged a tight embrace and headed back toward the house, so they could get cleaned up and be presentable for their "Madi Gras" celebration, just a few hours away.

How are we alike?
How are we different?

Psalm 118:24

"This is the day the Lord has made;
let us rejoice and be glad in it."

adi stood in front of her bathroom mirror, smiling contently as Mom carefully finished curling the last few ringlets of her golden-brown locks. "A special day calls for especially beautiful hair," Mom stated, reaching into the vanity's side drawer and pulling out a thin, decorative headband adorned with a cluster of metallic purple, green, and gold curlicues. "Is this the one you were wanting to wear?" she asked, sliding it gently onto Madi's head.

"Yep…that's it!" Madi replied. "I wore this same one at my very *first* 'Madi Gras' celebration, didn't I?"

"You surely did…and on every Adoption Day since! These exact colors are used at another celebration that occurs right around this same time each year, called '*Mardi* Gras.' That's where we got the idea to call *your* special day 'Madi Gras'…get it? The whole family will be dressed up tonight in their decorative masks, with layers of beaded necklaces dripping from their necks. We'll certainly be a sight to see!" Mom giggled. "Do you remember what the purple, green, and gold colors actually stand for?"

Madi thoughtfully looked up toward the ceiling, trying to remember, but then shook her head, "What do they mean again, Mommy?" she asked.

"The *purple* symbolizes "justice"; Jesus's passion and suffering before He died on the cross for *all* of our sins—past, present, and future. The *green* symbolizes "faith," renewal, and the belief that those who are faithful will be rewarded with everlasting life through Christ Jesus. Jesus loved us *so much* that He was willing to die on the cross so that we could be forgiven our sins and live *forever* in Heaven with God. And the *gold* symbolizes "power," a reminder that God is *always* present in our life, from beginning to end. Oh, that reminds me…I've got one last finishing touch to make your outfit complete. Follow me…"

Mom led Madi back into her bedroom and over to the dresser, where she opened up the top of Madi's heart-shaped, pink-satin jewelry box. From it, she pulled a small square box. She slowly eased the top off the box to reveal a delicate, purple-winged butterfly pin nestled inside. "This, too, belonged to your grandma Peggy. I know she's smiling down on us right now, and is delighted that you'll be wearing this today." Mom pinned the sparkly brooch onto Madi's dress, just above her heart. "You're all set, Muffin. Let's get your father, and head downstairs…It's time to go!" Mom said, excitedly.

The three hopped into the car and headed out to meet the rest of the family at one of Madi's favorite restaurants, one that was well matched for celebrating her "Madi Gras" festivity. "How long until we get there?" Madi asked, with eager anticipation. She could hardly wait to see her nana and granddaddy, Aunt Lisa and Uncle Bill, and her two older cousins.

"Soon, Sweetheart, real soon," Dad replied. "Hey…who do you think is going to find the baby in the king cake this year and get to wear the crown?" Daddy asked Madi.

"Me, I hope!" Madi laughed aloud as she remembered how last year, it was her *daddy* who bit down into his slice of cake and was surprised to find the small plastic baby hidden inside his mouthful!

The king cake was another tradition her family shared on "Madi Gras," and everyone enjoyed the chance of being the sole person to discover the hidden baby Jesus inside the cake, naming the finder as "king" of the party. The crowned victor was meant to represent one of the three wise men who had traveled the desert to bring gifts to the infant Jesus after His birth, and the winner often got to take home whatever leftovers there were of the sweet treat as well. The oval-shaped coffee cake consisted of nuts, sweet pieces of fruit, and a yummy custard filling. Again, Madi couldn't resist the delicious icing atop the cake, decorated in squiggly lines of green, purple, and gold. "I love it—yummy!" Madi proclaimed. "What's *your* favorite part of the cake, Mommy?" she asked.

"Definitely the little bits of fruit throughout," Mom shared. "The fruit pieces are yet another reminder for us, representing the nine visible 'Fruits of the Spirit' that reveal God's active love working within those who believe in Him."

"Oh, I know what they are!" Madi interrupted. "I learned these in chapel at school. Let's see…" she continued; holding up a finger for each one, she recited, "they are love, joy, peace, patience, kindness, goodness, faithfulness, gentleness, and…" Madi paused a moment to remember what the last one was.

"Self control!" Dad chimed in, smiling. "I certainly hope I'll be able to show some self-control tonight and not eat too much of that cake!" They all exploded in laughter, just as they pulled into the restaurant's parking lot.

The family enjoyed their dinner and celebration together, taking turns going around the table, sharing treasured memories of Madison's adoption and giving thanks for the blessing Madi was to them. She felt so special from everyone's affection, as well as the abundance of gifts she had received. She couldn't help but think how *doubly* exciting it was that she got presents on her birthday *and* on "Madi Gras," too!

John 3:16
"For God
so loved the
world that He gave
His one and only
Son, that whoever
believes in Him shall
not perish but have
eternal life."

Back at home, Mom and Dad began folding down Madi's bed covers while she changed into her nightgown and climbed tiredly into bed. "Did you have a good time tonight, Honey?" Mom asked, assisting Madi in removing the jeweled crown from her head and the two remaining beaded necklaces from around her neck, then placing them on her nightstand.

"It was positively PURR-fect," Madi said appreciatively. "Thank you for the best day ever!"

"Did you like all of your presents?" Daddy asked.

"Absolutely!" Madi responded.

Mom and Dad scooted in close on either side of Madi as she rested her head on the pillow and snuggled her "Baby Bunny" tightly under her chin. They clasped hands and closed their eyes, while Dad prayed, "Dear Lord, thank You again for this amazing day, and for the blessed gift of our daughter, Madison. We are so thankful that You chose *us* to be her parents, and we will continue to give You *all* the praise and glory for her creation and talents. We will give You thanks daily for her uniqueness and treasure her as a rare jewel You crafted with Your perfect hand. Please continue to protect her and keep her safe. In Your Son Jesus's Name, Amen."

Mom and Dad took turns kissing Madi goodnight, tucking the covers in tightly around her, and together they walked toward her bedroom door to turn out the light. Madi said softly and lovingly to her parents, "Good night, I love you…"

"Good night, Madi, we love you *more*…" they whispered, gently shutting her bedroom door.

Through the door they heard Madi's sweet voice respond faintly once more, *This I know for sure…* I love *you*, Mommy and Daddy, *mostest of all*…"

What do you love about me?
Share my adoption story with me…

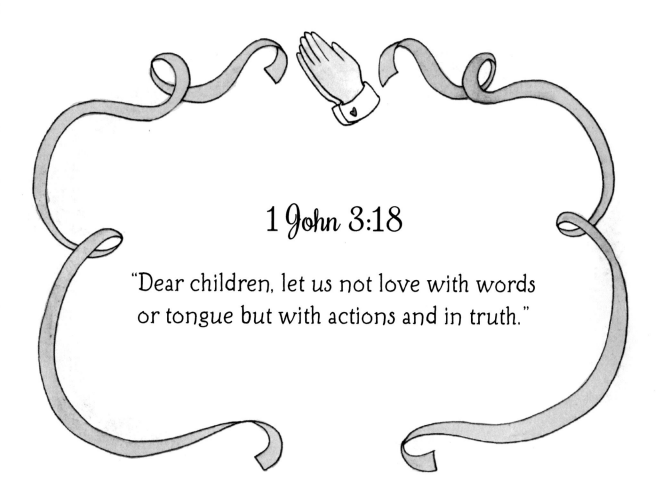

1 John 3:18

"Dear children, let us not love with words
or tongue but with actions and in truth."

Share *your* personal story, how you celebrate your child's adoption day, special family
traditions and photos, and/or how this book has enriched your time together~
Email: *ThisIKnowForSure@yahoo.com*

Enjoyed this book? Please recommend it to your friends and family.
Be a blessing…post your uplifting comments and "Like" the story on Facebook~
Search: *This I Know For Sure*

Fill Up My Love Cup!

Parents, use this page to journal your fondest memories of your child's adoption,
what makes him or her uniquely special, how your child has blessed your family,
and your deepest desires for his or her future...

How you grew in my heart ~

What I love about you ~

How we're alike ~

How you're uniquely you ~

What you've taught me ~

How you changed my life ~

Our family traditions ~

My dreams for you ~

Your adoption story ~

_____

_____

_____

_____

_____

_____

_____

_____

Insert
Family Photo
Here

~ 10 Ways to Celebrate Adoption & Family ~
by Stacie Cahill, MSW / www.helpstartshere.org

1. Encourage your child to design his or her own "LOVE CUP," which you will fill with words of praise and encouragement. Each child will enjoy decorating the cup with stickers, markers, etc. He or she will feel special and will look forward to checking the "Love Cup" for notes from Mom or Dad.

2. Remember to hug or kiss your child daily, as he or she will gain from physical contact.

3. Spend at least two hours per week of quality one-on-one time with your child, in which no other people are present. Your child will know that he or she is important and will enjoy the individual attention.

4. Write a short story or make up a song concerning your child's birth or adoption experience. Read the story or sing the song to your child.

5. Remember to give your child at least one affirmation or acknowledgement on a daily basis.

6. Laugh with your child. Communication through laughter will strengthen the parent-child bond. Comedy movies and a good joke book may help to encourage laughter.

7. Watch home videos and look at old pictures of your child's birth or early years, if you have them. The child will benefit by sensing your excitement regarding his or her life.

8. Make a special dinner together. Allow your child to choose the menu and assist with the meal preparation.

9. Journal with your child. Encourage your child to choose a journal and write anything there that he or she would like to share with you. After you read these notes, write back concerning special happenings in your own life. This is a great way to openly communicate with your child, and will help to foster feelings of security and trust. Save the journals and share them with your child when he or she is older. The journals will be especially meaningful to an adult child, and will be a gift to be treasured forever!

10. Interview your child once a year with a home video recorder, asking questions regarding any area of interest. Perhaps you will want to review his or her likes and dislikes. It will be meaningful to capture your child's very own thoughts concerning special events in his or her life.

~ About the Author ~

Former special education teacher, now stay-at-home mom to her seven-year-old daughter, Madison Faith, Karen Capson and her husband, Greg, recently celebrated fifteen years of marriage. Together, they endured countless heartbreaks along their journey to become parents, from unexplained infertility and the loss of three pregnancies to the devastating passing of Greg's mother from breast cancer in 2005. Through these struggles, they grew stronger as a couple and developed a solid foundation in their Christian faith, which ultimately guided them to relinquish their own pursuit of parenthood and put their lives in the capable hands of their Almighty Father. They prayed diligently for eight years, asking Him to grant them the *one* request that they had believed impossible, even through modern medicine…to have a child to call their own. Through God, they learned that ALL things are possible!

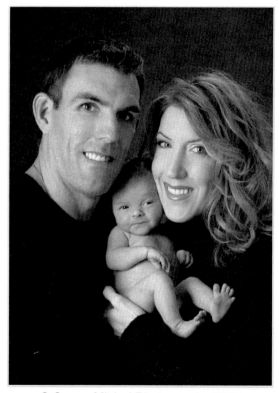

© Susan Michal Photography 2005

Their hearts were opened to the idea of adoption in the latter part of 2003, and their prayer requests were brought to fruition with the birth of their daughter in 2005. The local adoption was finalized in early 2006, where the celebration of Madison's Adoption Day sparked the onset of a new family tradition, also known as "Madi Gras." Since then, Karen has become a strong advocate for adoption, leading several friends not only to contemplate this alternate path to parenthood, but to see their dream become a reality by walking them through the adoption process.

Karen's positive experience with adoption, and belief that God specifically designed their child uniquely for them, inspired her to write her first children's book, "This I Know For Sure…." What began with the sole purpose of giving their daughter, Madison, a lasting "snapshot" of her adoption, evolved into a greater faith-led mission to write a story that would stand as a testament to God's intricate and purposeful plan for *every* child.

Madison & Family ~ Mother's Day 2013

Made in the USA
Lexington, KY
04 October 2017